ACTIVE
CITIZENSHIP
TODAY

Supporting Groups That Fight for Fairness and Equality

Jackie F. Stanmyre

Cavendish Square

New York

Published in 2018 by Cavendish Square Publishing, LLC
243 5th Avenue, Suite 136, New York, NY 10016

Library of Congress Cataloging-in-Publication Data

Names: Stanmyre, Jackie F.
Title: Supporting groups that fight for fairness and equality / Jackie F. Stanmyre.
Description: New York : Cavendish Square Publishing, 2018. |
Series: Active citizenship today | Includes index.
Identifiers: LCCN ISBN 9781502629340 (library bound) | ISBN 9781502629326
(pbk.) | ISBN 9781502629333 (6 pack) | ISBN 9781502629357 (ebook)
Subjects: LCSH: Equality--United States--Juvenile literature. | Fairness--Juvenile literature.
| Discrimination--United States--Juvenile literature. | Social justice--Juvenile literature.
Classification: LCC HM821.S68 2018 | DDC 305.800973--dc23

Editorial Director: David McNamara
Editor: Fletcher Doyle
Copy Editor: Nathan Heidelberger
Associate Art Director: Amy Greenan
Designer: Joe Parenteau
Production Coordinator: Karol Szymczuk
Photo Research: J8 Media

The photographs in this book are used by permission and through the courtesy of: Cover B Christopher/
Alamy Stock Photo; p. 4 Rawpixel.com/Shutterstock.com; p. 6 Chris from Paris/Shutterstock.com; p. 8
Patrickheagney/iStockphoto.com; p. 8 Jaren Jai Wicklund/Shutterstock.com; p. 10 Brian Mitchell/Corbis/
Getty Images; p. 11 John Birdsall/Alamy Stock Photo; p. 12 SolStock/iStockphoto,com; p. 14 Jupiterimages/
Creatas/Thinkstock; p. 15 Owen Franken/Corbis/Getty Images; p. 16 Michael Steele/Getty Images;
p. 17 Ktaylorg/iStockphoto.com; p. 18 SolStock/E+/Getty Images; p. 19 Monkeybusinessimages/
iStock/Thinkstock; p. 20 Jim West/Alamy Stock Photo; p. 22 Fstop123/E+/Getty Images; p. 23 Denise
Truscello/WireImage/Getty Images; p. 24 FatCamera/iStockphoto.com; p. 25 Courtesy You Can
Play; p. 26 (top) Ales-A/iStockphoto.com, (bottom) Monkey Business Images/Shutterstock.com.

Printed in the United States of America

CONTENTS

1

People in Need

You might have heard your parents say, "Life's not fair." But what does that mean? In a fair world, everyone is treated equally. Everyone gets what he or she needs. Unfortunately, that does not happen. You can see many ways the world is not fair.

Opposite: Everyone should be treated equally and get what they need.

There are groups and organizations that help. Sometimes children may feel they cannot make a difference. They feel they cannot help. One way to help is to support groups that fight for fairness and equality.

Hunger

Healthy children eat three meals every day. Not all children are so lucky. One out of every six children in the United States goes hungry. Some families don't have enough money. Some families don't

Many children go to school feeling hungry.

know about healthy eating. It is not the children's fault. They can learn ways to be healthier.

JEFFREY GETS HELP

A boy named Jeffrey lives in central Florida. He lives with his grandmother and four siblings. There is not enough food for everyone.

Jeffrey eats breakfast and lunch for free at school. He takes home fruits and vegetables when some are left over. Once a month, a church brings two boxes of food to Jeffrey's apartment.

Jeffrey wants to work on motorcycles when he grows up. He knows he needs the right food to grow stronger and smarter.

Hunger hurts children in many ways. Kids who are hungry get sick more. They miss more school. They have a harder time listening. Their grades are worse. Hungry children are less likely to graduate from high school.

Disabilities

Many children have a **disability**. They may have trouble hearing, talking, or seeing. They may need help walking. They may have a hard time behaving

Hungry children get sick more often than well-fed kids.

around other kids. They may not be able to care for themselves.

Children may be born with a disability. They may become disabled from a sickness or accident. Life can be harder for children with disabilities. They do not always get the help they need.

Steps are a big obstacle for people in wheelchairs.

Making a Difference

Many children with disabilities need extra help. A child who cannot walk may need a wheelchair. He or she may need wheelchair ramps to get into buildings.

Lydia lives in Tennessee. She uses a wheelchair. Lydia has a disorder, or illness, that stunted her development.

When Lydia was ten, a man noticed she was having trouble. His name was Tom Mitchell. He saw Lydia was having difficulty getting in and out of her house.

A store donated wood. Tom Mitchell used it to build a ramp. Now, Lydia can get in and out of her house more easily.

Different Needs

Children who cannot see need special books. These books use a special language called **Braille**. With Braille, each letter is represented by a pattern of

Blind children can read books written in Braille.
Special teachers help them learn Braille.

Supporting Groups That Fight for Fairness and Equality

raised dots. Children can feel the letters. These children also need teachers who can help them learn Braille.

Access to Play

Children are not always treated equally when it comes to playing games. Sometimes this happens on a single playground. A girl or boy is not allowed to play soccer or kickball. This isn't fair.

Sometimes whole groups of children, like girls, are left out. This is **discrimination**.

Being excluded from games can make kids very sad.

2

Places That Help

There are many organizations and programs to help children. People in these groups try to make the world more fair.

The National School Lunch Program feeds children. It started in 1946. It gives lunch to millions of students every day. These lunches give children good **nutrients**. Programs like this exist all over the world.

Opposite: National programs provide students with a healthy lunch.

The School Breakfast Program offers free breakfast to children. This way the children can start their day with a good meal. This will give them energy. It will help them focus at school.

Food Pantries

Children and families can get food at food pantries. Every state has food pantries. You can find locations at http://www.foodpantries.org.

Food pantries give groceries to families that don't have enough money to pay for them.

At food pantries, families that don't have money to buy food get groceries. Churches, mosques, and temples also have food for families.

Supporting Disabilities

The Arc is a huge organization. It started with just a few parents in the 1950s. The parents had children with disabilities. They wanted more for their children. At that time, there were no programs for children with disabilities.

Now The Arc has groups in seven hundred states or towns. The Arc makes sure children with disabilities and their families have support. The organization helps to make sure children can be involved in their communities.

Children with disabilities like to play sports.

Helping Disabled Children

Children with disabilities may not be able to play games with their **able-bodied** friends. The Adaptive Sports Foundation helps children age five and older who have disabilities. The foundation helps children with disabilities to ski, snowboard, and do yoga. They even can train for the Paralympics.

People with disabilities can still be top athletes. They can compete in the Paralympics.

That is an **international** athletic competition similar to the Olympics.

Against Bullying

Children with disabilities may be bullied at school. Children with disabilities are two to three times more likely to be bullied. They may be picked on because they look different or move differently. It may happen because of the way they talk. This is not fair treatment.

Organizations such as the PACER National Bullying Prevention Center can help everyone.

Children should be nice to people who are different. They should treat them fairly.

WHAT IS BULLYING?

All kinds of bullying can cause pain to the victims.

Bullying hurts someone with words or actions. The person being hurt has a hard time stopping the bully. Examples of **physical** bullying are hitting, shoving, and tripping. Examples of **emotional** bullying are name-calling, harsh teasing, **excluding** someone, or starting rumors.

Children with disabilities can learn to stand up for themselves. Children without disabilities can learn why they must treat everyone equally and fairly.

Access to Play

For a long time, girls were not allowed to play sports like boys were. A law was passed in 1972. Part of it was Title IX. This law makes sure girls get equal access to sports at school.

Not everyone gets treated fairly. Children who are gay, lesbian, bisexual, transgender, or queer often feel excluded. They think they must hide who they are on athletic fields. Sometimes they do not play at all. A group called

Girls were not always allowed the chance to play sports at school.

You Can Play is changing that. The group believes all children should feel safe to be themselves in the locker room, on the field, or in the stands.

Making Things Fair

Children may notice that the world is unfair and unequal. These children can do a lot to help others.

Food Banks

Children and their families can **volunteer** at food banks. A volunteer works without getting paid.

Opposite: Volunteering is a good way to help others.

Helping at food banks allows needy families to get healthy food. There is a website for people who want to volunteer. Ask a parent to visit http://www .feedingamerica.org/take-action/volunteer. They can look up nearby food banks. Volunteers sort and repack food or collect food at food drives.

A woman named Mary was hungry as a child. Now she volunteers for a food bank every week. She wrote about her work on the Feeding America website.

She says there are many ways you can help. Find a job you like. Then put your heart into the work. You will help your community. You will feel good.

"You'll make a positive difference

It feels good to help those who are hungry and others in need.

not only in the life of someone who needs it, but also in your own," Mary says.

Support Children with Disabilities

Easterseals is a national organization. It helps children and adults with disabilities.

Easterseals holds an event every year. It is called Walk With Me. The event raises money across the country. It supports people living with disabilities. It tells others about the needs of people with disabilities. Walk With Me raises

Walk With Me events raise money for people with disabilities.

millions of dollars to help families with disabilities.

Ask an adult to find an Easterseals Walk With Me near you. You can raise money and show support for children with disabilities.

Everyone should be able to play sports.
Encourage and respect others.

You Can Play

All children should be able to play sports and games. Make sure you don't exclude boys or girls who want to participate.

If you want to support this message, help the You Can Play Project. Create a You Can Play video with your friends. Post it to the You Can Play Project website. Show that you **encourage** everyone to respect each other.

Children can also work with adults on a You Can Play event. It can be held at your school. This could be a **fundraiser**. Everyone can play a game or a sport together.

You Can Play events like the one shown here raise funds for progams that are inclusive.

Donating

Some families are able to donate money to causes. They can give to groups that support fairness and equality. There may be a cause you believe in. Ask your parents if they are able to make a donation. This money helps the world become fairer and more equal.

Run a Bake Sale

The No Kid Hungry organization helps hungry children. It has a way for everyone to get involved.

Baking is a fun way to make sure that no kid goes hungry.

Children and their families can hold a bake sale. It will raise money for nutritious food for kids. No Kid Hungry teaches families how to cook healthy, affordable meals. Money from many bake sales adds up quickly.

To learn about how to run a bake sale, visit https://www.nokidhungry.org. Scroll down to "Bake Sale for No Kid Hungry." You and your friends could have fun looking up healthy recipes. Ask a grown-up for help. You will raise money for a good cause.

Bake sales can make a lot of money for a good cause.

Glossary

able-bodied Not handicapped or disabled; physically and mentally healthy.

Braille A system of raised dots or points used to represent letters that can be read by touch.

disability A physical or mental handicap, affecting strength or physical or mental ability.

discrimination Treatment for or against a person based on group, class, or category, such as race or gender.

emotional Of or related to feelings or expressions.

encourage To inspire with courage, spirit, or confidence.

excluding Not allowing someone to be part of an activity or group.

fundraiser An event that collects money to give to an organization or a cause.

international Involving two or more countries.

nutrient Something in food that is good for your body.

physical Of or relating to the body.

volunteer A person who performs a service willingly and without pay.

Find Out More

Books

Thomas, Pat. *Don't Call Me Special: A First Look at Disability*. A First Look At ... Hauppauge, NY: Barron's Educational Series, 2005.

Organizations

The Arc

https://www.thearc.org

This group wants to help people with intellectual and developmental disabilities to "achieve with us."

Easterseals

http://www.easterseals.com

Donate to Easterseals to help the disabled or learn where you can go on a Walk With Me.

No Kid Hungry

https://www.nokidhungry.org/problem/
hunger-facts

Find out the facts about hungry children and ways
to help them.

PACER Center

http://www.pacer.org/bullying

The PACER National Bullying Prevention Center
gives tips on how to end bullying.

You Can Play Project

http://www.youcanplayproject.org

LGBTQ athletes and their allies team up for respect.

Supporting Groups That Fight for Fairness and Equality

Index

Page numbers in **boldface** are illustrations.

About The Author

Jackie F. Stanmyre is a social worker and writer. As a children's book author, she has written for the Dangerous Drugs, Game-Changing Athletes, Primary Sources of the Abolitionist Movement, and It's My State series. Jackie lives in New Jersey with her husband and son.